The Cl...

Hunters Glen ES LMC
13222 Corona St.
Thornton, CO 80241-1162

by Karen Anderson

photographs by Kate Handley

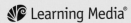
Learning Media®

Look at my pants.

Look at my shirt.

Look at my flower.

Look at my shoes.

Look at my wig.

Look at my hat.

Look at my face.

Look at me!